it's just a phase i'm going through

Ruby Trujillo

BookLeaf Publishing

Presentation by *BookLeaf Publishing*

Web: www.bookleafpub.com

E-mail: info@bookleafpub.com

ISBN: 9789357211680

First edition 2023

DEDICATION

to the states of change

ACKNOWLEDGEMENT

My true self is revealed to a few people in my life. To those who accept me as I am, I owe you so much.

Untitled 1

Hey there, mister moon
Why don’t you have a clue
That i'm in love with you
You're all mine Mr. moon

Every night, I dream of you
every night, I look at you

We have so much in common
It’s your heart that i'm robbin
I don’t need anybody
cuz you're the only heavenly body
That I need
the only one I need

You have always been there for me
While everyone in my life always leaves
My friends say it can't be
My family say I’m crazy
I don’t care,
I'll still run right back to you

I love you to the moon and back
There is no way i'm going back
To all the past lovers
And being sad

You're all alone up there
And I’m all alone down here
Lets us be alone together
Let us grow old together

Untitled 2

Aphrodite
Give me your strength
Give me your strength
Today

I'd be lying
If I didn't care
Of the lovers that went
Away

They grow uninterested
Unbothered
Make them feel as though
They're underwater

Drowning in my love today
Today
pearls illuminate
your face, with grace

Aphrodite
Give me your love
Give me your love
One day

Untitled 3

Who am I
Who are you
Staring into the blue

I don't know what to do
Because I feel like a fool

I am lost out at sea
I'm my own enemy

And I think i'm okay
I've seen worse, I'm afraid

Captain of my ship
I need no assistance

There is no one that I trust
It's the feeling of my rust

I'm sure there's a way
I will find it one day

Untitled 4

As the moon
As the wolf
As my old self

It aint ever going to be like it once was

As the judge
As the child
As my demons

I pray to remember the semblance

As the dust
As the sigh
As my seasons

I'll stay in my bed til I stop dreaming

Untitled 5

I stare at you all day
Hoping you would
At least just maybe (come by)(my way)
I'm just here all alone
I lay on my cobweb pillow,
I wait all day for you

Can you even see me?
Or do I just scare you away?
I know that I seem beastly
But believe that I am your prey

I know I'm way too small
I know my legs are long
But when you see me bounce
You can see how I am strong

When I spin my webs for the day
Human you keep my mind at bay

I should be scared but with you
I can't think
My defense mechanisms all go away in a blink
I don't know if we'll make it work

But I hope
That one day
you'll be attracted to this lonely arachnid

Untitled 6

I’d move to some place ancient
In Iceland or the woods

Somewhere where I'd die painting
Where I would be understood
Where no one be able to find me
Where no one could hurt me again

I'd have a warm little cottage
Filled with sweet berries n cheese
I wouldn’t care how I looked like
And I wouldn’t need anything

I’d never care about people
Because people just walk out the door

Untitled 7

I bombed that test
got rejected from that job again
I'm in such unrest,
I feel bad whenever I complain

I'm in constant grievance
Every day,
I’m losing people
Every day
It's all my fault
Always

Did I piss off a witch?
Did I break too many mirrors ?
Am I too much of a bitch?
Why don’t things seem clearer?

I'm a host of all the bad dreams
I dream about my ex
I dream about no control
I wish my thoughts would just deflect

My brain supposed to be on my team
But it keeps scoring in the wrong goal

I think I pissed off a witch
And I broke too many mirrors
I probably am a bitch
When do things get clearer?

Untitled 8

why should i hate myself
oh, your lies still sit on my minds shelf
is it a crime, to exist as I am
in this circuitry, it don’t mean much to me

that you don't even hear
no, you don't even see
no, you don't even care for me

oh, yes all my shelves are full, and I am
completely capable
i don't care, if you don't like how I look
damn my dependency, it means the world to me

the way you think of me
the way I talk and breathe
the way my spirit bleeds

Untitled 9

Aquí todo el mundo camina
Para siempre cuando nuestros termina
Many don't know this but,
all of our pains and beauties have been
experienced before
By our ancestors, with their own personal wars

With temporary success
With long years of struggle and contempt
And yet
We exist
Within our truest sense
With long years of tradition and what was once
merely dreamt

Untitled 10

My heart is closed for business
For now and for forever

No more kiss transactions
No more inventory checks on my soul
Sold out of all my admiration
With no more hands to hold

Rip all the receipts you have
I have filed for heart bankruptcy

If you need to return anything,
My kiss, my hugs, my identity
Throw it into the sea

And I'll make sure
Aphrodite will recycle it for me

Untitled 11

Sunflower, ray of sun
You are the only one
Who's soft and sweet to me
Under this garden tree

Oh so nice, so bright

Sunflower, open wide
Wide as the deep blue sky
I like to just sit by
Soak up your golden eyes

Oh the time, we spend
Goes fast and then
My tears I lend,
Your eyes they mend.

Sunflower, stay right there
I'll bring by my old lawn chair
I'll stay until you need to bear
The sun for another year

Oh, take care my friend
As the sun descends

Untitled 12

I’m your jester
I'll do anything
Do anything
to make you laugh

Please remember
All my cunning jokes on your behalf

My king
I know it's quite unseen
To love and cherish you
like a queen

And yet
With pleasure
I have jeered and danced
Fueled by foolish romance
At your worn knee

Life is one big joke
But I don’t know what’s funnier
The rope upon my weak neck
Or your face with no ulterior

Untitled 13

It’s not serious
I know, I know

But, I think I looked too long
I think I kissed too long

I can’t be casual
Cool or concise

My brain, it spins along
All of my oxygen, all my thoughts

Untitled 14

I know
I said I wouldn’t chase
But her blinded soul
Makes my head and heart race

She's a darling starred girl
Up above from heavens space
And I quite like the idea
Of her close by, close just in case

Oh, my Jessica
Like a rabbit
I will make her laugh
It's a habit
I will kiss her thoughts
 kiss her sadness
She's a work of art, mighty lapis
There's no need for doubts, no more drabness

Untitled 15

She was sitting right next to me
The perfect memory

For me

I want her right next to me
Falling asleep with me

If only

She's painfully beautiful
Whatever shed ask I'd do

Oh yes

She doesn’t quite notice me
She’ll sing at my eulogy

breathless

My compass is conflicted
I think about her close
I just want to kiss her
But I'm weeds to her pink rose

Untitled 16

i don't think you'd even care if i was run over by
a bus
by a bus
and i
i don't think you'd even care if my heart were to
combust

i don't care but i do
the way walk into a room

And it's not fair but it's true
how warmly I care about you

Untitled 17

Come and see about me
Tell me what you perceive to be
It comes to you so easily
The lessons, pitfalls so free
Or so it seems

It seems like everyone lives a life
With glamor and glorious surprise
I want that, tell me the price
With no fear, no second thoughts, with vice
With some vice

Change my mind
Change these eyes
 Look within
What's inside?

What goes on in that mind of yours
Share your confidence and joys
Id take it all id steal it if I could
My mind's green filled to the teem
Of you

Goodness, you're glowing just like the gods

Wisdom and wit inside your walls
I've been walking down empty halls
Here I stay, oh here I stay, in awe
Break me down
Break me down

Can I change
My fucking brain

Untitled 18

She rides all by her own
She knows no place is home
She goes off to the west
To find her place of rest

Dusty landscapes, the blisterin sun
She can escape, away she will run
The past still haunts her
It left her all undone

She drunk her red eyes And drowned in it good
She can disguise, her ladyhood
No one minds her, it's all understood

The campfire burns inside her soul
A cowboy with no place to go
Her answers lie within the stars
But she's blinded
she's blinded
she's blinded

This ol cowboy finds gold with her eyes
That western magic, the prize winning skies
It's so tragic, all she can do see behind

"I have this life now, free from demise,
But I miss my baby, my sweet angel eyes

She doesn't know it, but she's missed by her love
They've been broken, by fear from above
She hopes she'll come back, back to her arms

A cowboy with no place to go

Her answers lie within her eyes
But she's blinded,
she's blinded
she's blinded

Untitled 19

I like when you hold me
In your arms enfold me

Softer lips even softer words and
You tell me that we should
Meet more often

I like when you told me
You liked to sit on roofs and see

Clouds drift along blushing skies
You make me blush in the dead of night
I hide secrets inside my mind
prayin you'd never leave

Untitled 20

I’m sick or running
Sick of chasing
Sick of turning around

I don't know who I was
Or who I am before it went down

I sent the invites
Sent the spiked sprites
Sent my idling eyes

I’m sick of pulling
sick of asking
Sick of playing the clown

Untitled 21

amor de la noche donde vas
tu tienes mi corazon y maz

please dont leave like this, we can talk
work it through amor, work with chalk

i dont want no lessons, no more thoughts
i want tender feelings , to evolve

you keep leaving me as i awake
broken hearted every morning without your face

You once told me that I was your star
our bodies inorbit, to revolve

amor de la noche donde vas
tu tienes mi corazon y maz

www.ingramcontent.com/pod-product-compliance
Lightning Source LLC
Chambersburg PA
CBHW051755130826
49812CB00033B/1170
9789357211680